GESTALT

and

THE WISDOM OF THE KAHUNAS

Bethal Phaigh

DeVorss & Company
P.O. Box 550
Marina del Rey, California 90291

ISBN: 0-87516-498-6

Library of Congress Catalog Card Number: 82-050928

Cover by P.'Emily Youngreen

Printed in the United States of America

With special thanks
to Claire and Robert Trotter

CONTENTS

To learn to use the High Magic one has to get rid of hindering complexes, and this is difficult to do for one's self. This difficulty will be met by group work in which one person assists another to unlock the path of contact with the High Self.

—Max Freedom Long
The Secret Science Behind Miracles, p. 191

INTRODUCTION

As a gestalt facilitator I believe it is my responsibility to be able to recognize "aboutism" and facilitate the switching of channels into the NOW, for in the NOW the magic of gestalt takes place, organically, as it does in meditation.

"Aboutism" represents separation in time from experience, the separation of observer/observed. Stuck in "aboutism" we need ever increasing stimulation, something a little bigger, a little more clever, a little more awesome to *observe*. In one of his poems Basho said:

> *"Climb Mount Fuji, oh snail,*
> *But slowly, slowly."*

Basho also observes, yet his observation is filled with the wonder of the moment: the snail's slowness contrasted with the mountain's immensity, Basho's awareness that the snail's direction is "up," its potential the top of the mountain. All these are "facts" in his awareness, coming together in a creative synthesis which is felt and expressed.

An analyst might only observe: a snail, its size, its speed, its colour, whether or not it is common to that place, etc. But the analyst would not likely be experiencing the magic of Basho's NOW.

There is nothing wrong with analysing and "talking about;" it has its place; I am doing that now. Its destructiveness comes from its overuse or misuse. Schools and universities especially foster its overuse, thereby conditioning students away from nowness. Most of us overuse aboutism, thinking we are communicating, while in reality we are only communicating facts, talking about something; ourselves, our problems, our feelings, our experiences, etc. Talking about is *not* expressing, and the difference is important in therapy for it is in the creative NOW that healing happens.

Eastern cultures have long been aware of the difference between aboutism and nowness: in meditation, noticing when a thought came in, and then, instead of getting hung up in thinking about, moving back into NOW awareness. They discovered that NOW awareness was the path to nirvana, the place to "be still and know that I am God." They developed disciplines such as yoga and tai-chi to facilitate this nowness.

We in the West have been so rewarded by our "figuring out" and "thinking about" that we were unaware of the imbalance we were creating in our lives. That is, until the loss of "centre" resulting from an overload of aboutism caused the counter-culture involuntarily to seek solutions. It was nature's way of dealing with the feeling of isolation which characterized the young people of the early 60's, particularly those from the large universities and high schools. The LSD era was not accidental: human nature will find a way, even though it is not aware of all the implications. The "flower children" discovered drugs and thereby tripped into the NOW.

An advantage of the drug experience was the discovery that there was another "space;" a disadvantage was that, as Baba Ram Dass so ably put it, "They discovered the spiritual room but that did not make them spiritual." It was like getting past the flaming swords into the Garden of Eden before they had cleared their maya, before they had "centred" enough to be citizens of the garden. Now that they'd had a glimpse of it, however, they wanted more. Some of them tried to become more spiritual by keeping themselves, with the aid of drugs, in the "spiritual room." By now most of them have realized that there is more to it than that, but having glimpsed Eden, they are searching for other ways.

Through Eastern meditation they discovered a discipline that they could incorporate into their lives through which they could strengthen their contact with the NOW. And the shamans, so adept at going to the NOW space, gained more significance within the society. Carlos Castaneda caught on like a prairie fire in a high wind. And into psychiatry at this time came the gestalt techniques of Fritz Perls.

An advantage of Fritz Perls' gestalt is that the NOW is expressed to "out there" and through this expression people have discovered a richer communication than was possible through the aboutism to which they had become accustomed. So many so-called spiritual communities became adept at the "inner NOW" techniques, but are still communicating with their culturally assimilated aboutisms. Rajneesh of India has effectively combined the "going in" NOW of meditation and the "going out" expressive NOW of gestalt, alternating these two with extreme sensitivity to the place of each.

In years of facilitating groups I have found that untrained people can quickly develop an ability to distinguish between NOW and aboutism while they are within the group. But out in the world where the patterns of aboutism are so strongly internalized, where, as Roszak says, "the technology rejects spontaneity, self-regulation, animal impulsiveness, as if they were so much poison in the body politic (. . .) preferring instead future goals and behaviour;"[1] out there it is more difficult to stay in the NOW. That is one reason the young people of the 60's had to get away from their parents and form their

1. Roszak, T. *The Making of a Counter Culture.* Doubleday, 1969, p. 198.

own communities. They did this organically, not understanding what was driving them.

Gestalt is one of the processes by which we can come to an appreciation of what was happening. It is, as well, a process whereby we may learn to stay centered in the NOW, even in a manipulative environment.

In this book I have explored various subjects important to the gestalt process, and enlarging on these, have followed each with relevant exercises, which hopefully will lead to richer communication. Many of the exercises are intended for group participation and I recommend the use of the book in this way.

Given this certainty that the Kahunas had known for thousands of years all the psychology we had come to know in the last few years, I became quite sure that their ability to perform feats of magic stemmed from their knowledge of important psychological factors not yet discovered by us.

—Max Freedom Long
The Secret Science Behind Miracles, p. 198

1

SYNTHESIS: THE WISDOM OF THE KAHUNAS, GESTALT, AND NLP*

I am frequently put into the category "gestalt therapist," and to a great extent this is valid. I recognize myself as a composite of many experiences and trainings, among them gestalt.

This book is written mainly to those with whom I have "worked" as a gestaltist. It is written as a resource book for them and any others who may find it valuable. All that I write will have been profoundly influenced by my shaman friends and by Findhorn in Scotland. What I have experienced from them has not contradicted, but has been an extension to, and a corroboration of what I learned from Fritz Perls in 1969. I owe a considerable debt of clarification to the work of Max Freedom Long and his translations from the original Huna (secret) language of the Hawaiian kahunas (healers). As I studied Max Freedom Long's perceptions of Huna healing, I recognized patterns I learned from Fritz Perls. This chapter, in fact the whole book, is a synthesis.

One of the points of similarity between the insights of the ancient kahunas and of Fritz Perls is their dividing of the personality into unique "selves:" the subconscious and the

* Neuro Linguistic Programming

reasoning self. The kahunas add another self: the High Self. It is interesting that, coming from such diverse backgrounds, the qualities and powers assigned to both the subconscious and reasoning selves are, for Fritz Perls and the kahunas, so similar. Fritz Perls is spoken of as a genius whose theories are having a profound influence on modern-day therapy. The kahunas have been around for what is, as yet, an immeasurable time.

Both Fritz Perls, and the kahunas as introduced to us by Max Freedom Long, recognize the importance of the subconscious. Fritz called the subconscious the *underdog*, the kahunas called it *low self*. Fritz said, "underdog always wins," the kahunas said low self is our *power source* and has control of all flows of body electricity and all thought forms after they are created. They said it manufactures life force (mana) for use by middle self and High Self.

The kahunas' middle self and Perls' topdog are the same. They are the intellectual self, the self that reasons. Max Freedom Long gave a lot of weight to the wisdom of middle self. Fritz Perls did not trust its counterpart, topdog, as much. I believe that this is partly due to the fact that in the 1960's (Fritz Perls' time) the world had become much more aware of the danger of rationalization than it had been at the time of Max Freedom Long's writings, (the first half of the century).

The third part of the personality, Huna's High Self, Fritz might have recognized as that moment when topdog and underdog integrated. He might have recognized it as intuition. But his work was concerned mainly with the integration itself. As to the importance of this, Huna would concur: Huna would say *middle self cannot contact High self without the support of low self.* The kahunas, as well as Fritz Perls, would first work on the integration of middle self and low self.

Following are some of the attributes of low self as given by Max Freedom Long; the gestaltist will find in them an almost exact counterpart to Fritz Perls' underdog.

MEMORIES: low self is the seat of memories.

EMOTIONS: low self is the seat of emotions.

NEED FOR SPECIFICS: low self cannot reason. Therefore orders must be specific.

PROGRAMS: low self does what it is programmed to do. It takes orders from middle self though it does not necessarily obey them.

COMPLEXES: low self contains "complexes" which must be dealt with before High Self can be reached. Frequently a memory pattern is planted without the consciousness of the middle self. Then it is hard to deal with since the rational self does not know its basis for actions in that area.

CLUSTERS OF MEMORIES: low self has clusters of memories, and we may be in touch with related memories by first getting in touch with one segment of the cluster, then allowing low self to bring the related ones to consciousness.

DREAMS: low self uses dreams to get a lot of these memories through to our middle (or rational) selves in order that some of our complexes may be examined.

POWER: low self refuses to give energy to a situation where it is being pushed by middle self against its will. Since low self is the power source for middle self, middle self is in need of low self's co-operation in order to get energy for anything middle self may want.

Since underdog, gestalt's counterpart to Huna's low self, is the seat of emotions and also represents our power source, it is well to examine what we do with our emotions. Running wild, they can be destructive. Ignoring them is impossible; underdog won't co-operate and will find its own way of expressing them. Deadening our emotions is deadening our power source or our contact with it. Trying to control them is to run the risk of having "rebel" underdog run its own program and any "juice" topdog has will be used up trying to police underdog. Integration of the two is of supreme importance.

Fritz Perls pioneered the two-chair method, in therapy, for integration. He would have us be our topdog on one chair, communicating with our underdog on a facing chair, moving back and forth in order to keep the two parts distinct and separate. Separating the two parts is a basic step in the integration process. It allows us to become familiar with each, and aware of where they do not come together.

Separating the two parts and having them work towards integration was what Mark Twain did with Huck Finn's conflicts. This process is much more evident in *Huckleberry Finn* than it is in *Tom Sawyer.* Since Huckleberry Finn was written years after Tom Sawyer, I see Mark Twain's use of this process as a learning he personally did in the time between the two books. He also spent time in Hawaii. Perhaps he was influenced by the kahunas?

In order to keep each part on its own chair, it is important to recognize both of them, to know the characteristics of each. Many of the characteristics of low self and its counterpart underdog have been given above. More needs to be said of topdog, so that topdog may be distinguished. Topdog is easily recognized as the lawmaker, full of shoulds and shouldn'ts; and by the use of judgments—good and bad, right and wrong. Topdog talks in aboutisms. These are topdog's tools. Be wary if you hear them coming from underdog's chair. Then you will know that that person has the two parts confused; and confusion is not integration.

Many of topdog's rights and wrongs, goods and bads, shoulds and shouldn'ts are valuable to us, yet each of us carries a load of them which are invalid, which do not help our spirit flow—and we are not consciously aware of many of these invalid ones. This is where underdog can help us. Discomfort makes us recognize that underdog is at work: underdog automatically responds with that feeling to whatever is invalid to it.

Remember, in Huna, low self (underdog) has a direct link to High Self. Should this channel be clear of complexes, underdog can know through it what is true and not true. Topdog has no link to High Self, but has to go through underdog to get to this "wisdom," this true-or-not-true. *It is not the same as topdog's right and wrong, good and bad,* although topdog will often act as if it were and will try to use this possibility to rationalize feelings.

Topdog will also act as if a rationalization were a feeling. "I feel that . . . ," is *not* a feeling, it is an opinion or a fantasy. Be aware of this trap. If something feels off centre, that is underdog trying to get through to us. Listen for your underdog's true-or-not-true, the one that is linked to the High Self. Develop it. Treasure it. Keep it pure of clutter from topdog. It comes to us in the still, small, quiet place, free of thinking abouts, and it is very personal. You can get to know it; you can become more familiar with it. Make sure it is not a rationalization; that it is not of the head, but of the heart; that it is not a judgment, but a feeling, a comfort or a discomfort.

Fritz Perls used to tell us: "Don't listen to the words; listen to the voice." This is another way you can distinguish topdog from underdog. Topdog *talks about* feelings, things, anything. Topdog's "talking about" voice will usually be monotone, boring. Underdog's voice will be alive with emotion.

If you are feeling bored, check for a preponderance of topdog communication and activate some underdog as you work with the two-chair method. I use a short signal, simply, "switch," when I hear someone getting bogged down on topdog's chair. This does not interrupt the flow. If the talking about is on underdog's chair, I say: "sounds like topdog is over here." In any case the two-chair method tends to be more effective with short statements and frequent movement from one chair to the other. This movement will put a brake on topdog's endless rationalization.

I also find value in listening for certain "talking-about" phrases which are a tip-off that topdog is operating: "It is . . . ," "they are . . . ," "you are . . . ," are all "talking-about" phrases. Underdog starts with: "I am . . . ," "I . . . ." When Moses heard the phrase: "I am that I am" coming from the burning bush, he recognized the great High Self, the ever NOW. Any description would have been talking aboutness; Moses experienced a direct link. Even "I am" however, can be a description: "I am tall." Listening for aboutness as opposed to expression requires practice, like learning to play music. The tips I am giving you are like learning to find the notes; they are not the music.

Although underdog has a "logic of its own," as Max Freedom Long says of low self, it cannot reason. To communicate this logic, its true-or-not-true, underdog uses a sensory message, comfort or discomfort, or a body movement, tension, etc. Explore these. Pay attention to them. Then let underdog bring from its memory bank any information relevant to the discomfort. Topdog may suggest other choices for dealing with the uncomfortable situation. If so, let underdog try them on to discover whether any of these choices feel valid. Beware, however, of being rationalized into a choice by topdog. Many of the discomforts with which we work have come from topdog rationalization: our own topdog, our parents', our teachers', etc.; and this programming of shoulds and shouldn'ts, goods and bads, rights and wrongs, has been done without adequte listening to underdog's comfort/discomfort.

There is another way to work with discomforts which goes deeper and takes practice and utilizes Huna's High Self. It is called Neuro Linguistic Programming (NLP). Richard Bandler and John Grinder have initiated it through studying films of gestaltists such as Fritz Perls and Virginia Satir at work. They familiarize us with the process in a book called *frogs into princes.*[2] I recommend this work to you. Here I quote their reframing outline for comment.

1. *Identify the pattern* (X) to be changed.
2. *Establish communication* with the part responsible for the pattern.
   (a) ''Will the part of me that runs pattern X communicate with me in consciousness?''
   (b) Establish the ''yes-no'' meaning of the signal.
3. *Distinguish between the behaviour*, pattern X, *and the intention* of the part that is responsible for the behaviour.
   (a) ''Would you be willing to let me know in consciousness what you are trying to do for me by pattern X?''
   (b) If you get a ''yes'' response, ask the part to go ahead and communicate its intention.
   (c) Is that intention acceptable to consciousness?
4. *Create new alternative behaviours* to satisfy the intention. At the unconscious level that part that runs pattern X communicates its intention to the creative part, and selects from the alternatives that the creative part generates. Each time it selects an alternative it gives the ''yes'' signal.
5. Ask the part ''Are you willing to *take responsibility* for generating the three new alternatives in the appropriate context?''
6. *Ecological check.* ''Is there any other part of me that objects to the three new alternatives?'' If there is a ''yes'' response, recycle to step 2 above.

As I mentioned before, this process would require practice. I recommend that you attend workshops with someone familiar with the process.

2. Richard Bandler and John Grinder: *frogs into princes*, page 160.

What interests me particularly about NLP is that Bandler and Grinder have studied films of gestaltists at work and have come up with a very close approximation of Huna healing as outlined by Max Freedom Long. In *The Secret Science at Work* (p. 84) Long says:

> *The kahunas believed in, and performed their miracles through contact with the third and highest form of consciousness in man (. . . .) that which we call for convenience, the High Self. (. . . .) The aka cord always connects the low self and the High Self after the fashion of a telephone wire. If the three selves are working normally and freely together, the low self (. . . .) at the request of the middle self (. . . .) can at any time call up the High Self by way of the aka cord and give it a message.*

Which appears to be what NLP, which has grown out of gestalt, is doing:

1. The "pattern" is related to Huna's "complexes" (fixations).
2. Middle self establishes communication with low self through low self's language, a sensory signal. Next we are after low self's motivation. What need is low self trying to fill?
3. Low self is able to communicate with words (thoughts), as long as we work with specifics, not rationalizations or generalities. We get information from low self in low self's language; it comes to us, we do not "figure it out." We check the results with middle self, the part which can formulate demands and initiate requests.
4. Remember low self can take orders from middle self. Now middle self is asking low self to go to High Self (the creative part) for other behavioral choices. (Middle self cannot go directly to High Self but must go through low self).

5. Find out if low self, the power source, will take responsibility for giving energy to these behavioral choices in the appropriate places. In other words, is low self at ease with this choice?

6. Final check for integration.

Exercises

The following exercises, although placed at the end of this chapter, are intended for use with the other chapters as well, as you find them appropriate. They are valuable as opening exercises. I recommend that you use only one or two of the exercises at a session except for topdog/underdog which could be practiced anytime for as long as you wish. Sometimes one of the other exercises makes a good break.

I

1. *FOR DEVELOPING FREEDOM OF EXPRESSION*

Ice-breaking (group) best done outside or in a large room.

(a) Form a circle.

(b) Take turns, one at a time, to be in the center of the circle. The person in the center does "action and sound" at the same time, whatever comes to them. After a minute or two, they stand in front of someone in the circle and that person copies them, exchanging places, then allows their action and sound to change as it will. After a minute or so they repeat the 'change places' process.

(c) Continue till everyone has had a turn. Be sensitive to when you feel tired and slow the action appropriately. Experiment all you like.

2. *FOR DEVELOPING AWARENESS*

Mirroring to music, in pairs, silently except for the music.

(a) Stand facing each other; move apart until arms are outstretched in front, fingertips not quite touching. Maintain position and drop arms.

(b) Close eyes and remain until you feel centred. Open eyes and wait for partner if partner's eyes are still closed.

(c) Mirroring each other, begin movement silently to the music, maintaining eye contact and your place on the floor, but allowing your body to respond to the music and your partner. Continue at least for ten minutes, longer if you wish. Start *very* slowly, and continue until you find your responses coming very easily. Usually I use a whole side of one tape.

3. *PRACTICE IN DISTINGUISHING BETWEEN "ABOUTISM" AND "NOW"*

Act out an incident, singly, within a group.

Act out an incident within your life as if you were there now.

"Now I am fourteen, standing on a corner of the street near my home. I see my home over there" (indicating). Put in awarenesses, sights, sounds, etc., always staying in the "I am." Now I am aware of ____ , now I am seeing ____ , now I am hearing ____ , now I am wondering ____ , etc. When there is another person in the scene, become that person. Now I am John. Give any information about that person in the "I am," just as you did for yourself. Move on your improvised stage to where John would be in relation to you. Express John's thoughts (or your fantasy of them) as well as the words you remember him saying. Express your own unspoken thoughts moving back to your own spot on the floor. Whenever John says something, be John saying it, from his own spot; in other words, create a real scene in the NOW, not a description. Have a separate spot for each part, even when you "become" a house, etc.

This exercise is difficult to do at first. Almost everyone slips into description: I was . . . , it was . . . , etc. The trick is to give specifics without describing. Let the other people in the group help you be aware of when you slip into talking about, rather than being, and gently call you back to being NOW.

This can be a fun exercise as well as an extremely valuable one to practice.

4. *TOPDOG/UNDERDOG*

Done singly within a group or singly with a friend as monitor.

Practice two-chair topdog/underdog communication, *first becoming familiar with the two parts as outlined in this chapter*. Have one chair for topdog, a facing one for underdog. Have someone listening in order to:

— help distinguish topdog from underdog

— notice when there is a need to switch chairs (if one part is monopolizing)
— check that both parts are on their own chairs.

For material with which to work take any current discomfort or indecision. Keep going until your two parts either:

— come to an agreement (integrate)

or:

— decide to go along with underdog (which is also an integration).

Note: Underdog does not make decisions. Underdog just *feels* about a new choice: "I'm into trying that" or "I'm not into trying that."

II

SENSORY AWARENESS

1. *THE FIVE SENSES* (Group Exercises)

(a) Seeing: take turns, one person at a time, to share with the group; "now I am seeing . . . ," taking care not to edit or think ahead.
Don't describe. Just name specifically; "a red curtain . . . ," "John's nose . . . ," whatever, giving only the facts needed for identification. To say "a beautiful red curtain" would introduce judgment. The idea is to practice being specific without being judgmental or descriptive.

(b) Hearing: do this one silently, sharing if you wish, at the end of the exercise. Sitting still for a few moments be aware of sounds.

(c) Smelling: recall a scent. Share what memories go with that scent. Try doing it in the "I am—" instead of descriptively.

(d) Touching: close your eyes. Move around the room keeping your eyes closed feeling the texture of other's clothes or skin. After the leader gives a signal, open your eyes and see if you can identify what you touched. Share what your responses were.

(e) Tasting: recall a taste you can't stand,
recall a taste you enjoy.
As you recall these, share this awareness with the group.

2. *THE BLIND WALK* done in pairs is an excellent followup to the above exercises. The "seeing" partner guides the "blind" partner for at least twenty minutes. I do not use blindfolds. I just explain that this exercise does not work well unless the blind partners keep their eyes closed this long. It takes this kind of time, usually, to develop enough trust so that the blind partners do not feel the need of their own eyes. At the end of twenty minutes the blind partner switches places with the seeing partner.

Since this also is a trust exercise, the seeing partner:

(a) Takes one hand or arm of the blind partner and works out pressure signals for tricky places, like steps.

(b) Needs to stay aware of anything that might break trust, like a tree branch that might touch the partner's face.

(c) Needs to be alert to anything which might interest the blind partner; scents, textures, etc.

(d) Could be aware of when the blind partner is ready to experiment with running. Running blind can be an exhilarating experience, but is not to be tried too soon, since developing trust is paramount.

(e) Both partners maintain silence. This eliminates both seeing and talking for the blind partner. Since seeing and talking are both used to objectify, this can be a valuable experiential exercise.

3. *THE "OHM" CIRCLE* (group)

(a) Form a circle; close your eyes and keep them closed throughout the exercise. Chanting "Ohm" or humming a tune of your choice, start moving through the centre of the circle to the other side. You will know when you are at the outside by the sound of the other voices. Then keep moving back through the centre again, humming, eyes closed.

(b) At a signal from the leader, form a circle again. Hold hands, fantasize whose hands you are holding.

(c) Open your eyes and share your experiences.

4. *PILLARS*—Space awareness (group)

Half of the group stands still as "pillars" at various places on the floor at least two feet from any other pillar. The other half of the group runs quickly, all at the same time, around the various pillars, not touching any of them. After a short while switch and have the runners be pillars.

5. *TO "FEEL" ENERGY* (group, in pairs)

Hold your hands with palms facing out; walk around the room meeting partners. Stand with palms an inch or so from your partner's. After a short while you may feel energy between your hands. You may sense it as heat, you may sense it as a buzz, sometimes it may feel like a cool breeze. When you are experiencing this energy, slowly move your hands away from your partner's, exploring where you lose the feel of energy. Then move back closer, feeling the intensity build. Move to another partner. No two are alike.

III

TO DEVELOP TRUST OR OVERCOME ANXIETY

1. *TAPPING* (pairs, silently)

   (a) Each person taps own face, neck, head, arms, shoulders, gently with the palms of their hands to feel which place and which pressure they enjoy more.

   (b) Now take turns tapping each other in the same places. Partners close eyes. At the conclusion of each series of tapping, stand facing your partner until partner opens eyes and makes contact with you.

2. *FALLING* (group)

Person stands on chair or table and falls into outstretched arms of people standing in two rows facing each other.

3. *FALLING IN CIRCLE* (group)

(a) Group forms circle, standing close. (About eight people.)

(b) One person goes into centre and closes eyes. Remaining straight but not rigid, the person falls backwards against the circle, keeping foot position throughout.

(c) Circle passes "body" back and forth, or around the circle.

(d) Conclusion, if desired: At a nod from someone, one person picks up feet of the person in the centre while all arms come under the person, raising his/her body horizontal to the floor. Now have the group start humming or quietly singing, rocking the person gently back and forth, then lower slowly to the floor. Once on the floor everyone could put their hands on the person for a moment, all raising hands off at the same time.

. . . a true hate has its own beauty, just like a true love—because beauty is concerned with truth.

—Rajneesh
Only One Sky, p. 22

2

OUR EMOTIONS AND WHAT WE DO WITH THEM

Since low self, our power station, is the seat of our emotions, it is important that we pay attention to our emotions and what we do with them. When we judge an emotion as bad, or as an addiction, we close the door to healing. *It is our responses we need to mistrust, not the emotion.* We need to "try on" various responses to the same emotion. Since low self has a direct link to High Self, it is possible for low self to discover which responses feel good to the total organism. If we are uncomfortable, then what low self may need is more choices of *how* to express the feeling. The place where people seem most limited in their choice of expression appears to be with the emotion of hating. I believe this is because they have been rationalized out of their right to this emotion:

"It's wrong to hate."
"Don't say that word."

So the emotion builds up until it has the potential of a bomb. Then something triggers it and it explodes, with very little choice as to how it is expressed. And this can be dangerous.

I have worked with people whose anger is so ready to explode, that they, as much as those around them, are afraid of that moment when explosion must surely happen. What they need is a way to dissipate the emotion safely; as Roszak suggests, finding a valid way of detonating the submerged charge of aggression rather than trying to defuse it.

Explosion is one symptom of lack of choice.

Put-down, judgment or criticism, intended to make the other person feel small, is another. This sets up a vicious circle: the more that people do these things, the less they are loved, the more they hate. Frustrated with their inability to love and be loved, they turn their anger out, trying to hurt someone, or they turn their anger in, into killing patterns within their own bodies, patterns such as cancer.

Depression, deadness, is another. We may become so adept at controlling an emotion that we are able, continually, to put it down ↓. But the emotion continues there, suppressed but needing expression ↑. So our energy is used up going nowhere ↕. Deadness. Depression.

Suicide follows depression, the pushed down feelings turned on self. The explosion is in, rather than out. What would have been strong enough feelings to commit murder, now become strong enough to commit suicide.

When I find people who have suicidal tendencies, the first place I work is with getting them to take the right to the feeling of hate. This is very difficult for them to do. Most of their problem comes from invalidating that feeling, and their belief system is so rigid that there is no way low self will give them any choice except the one they are using. So I work with this "complex," as Huna would call it.

I start by exploring the belief, if they have it, that it is invalid to hate another person; if we explore their *feeling* we find that what they really hate is not the person but something that the person has done, something in a *specific* place, with a *specific* action, at a specific *time*. So, although it may appear to be the person we hate, we may discover it is really an action or a series of actions by that person that triggered our feeling. For me, a person's belief that it is invalid to hate another person is indeed valid. It is also valid to hate something someone has done.

Loaded feeling. Often we have carried resentments from similar actions by that person, or even from similar actions committed by others, until our feeling has become "loaded" with all the pick-ups. Since the individuals with whom we are working need specifics to clear a feeling, ask them to try to pick one instance out of the load and try to clear that. Have them state all the *specifics*— where, when, how the discomfort started, exactly. Then say "I hate you for *that*" and see how it feels.

Any incident cleared this way will clear other incidents of similar weight and likeness. There is no need to go through all of them. Now the person with whom I am working has another choice: not "I hate you," but "I hate you for . . . " (the specific). Or, "I hate *that*" (after they have got in touch with the specifics). It is always important to get in touch with the specifics when clearing a negative emotion. Otherwise it won't "clear."

With this awareness that it is an *action*, not the person, that they hate, they may begin to detonate their "bomb." They will detonate some of their bomb even with the pickups, if these come first; but they can demolish it with the original specific. Low self can help them find it. If we are open to it, low self will float to the top the memory we need. If we are not very open, low self may use a dream to get through. The murderers, the violaters, in a dream, are your own buried resentments trying to get through. See the chapter on dreams for how to detonate these.

Every connected release or expression of "I hate *that*" will result in healing which will be immediately felt. But it must be connected to the low self, to the emotion, in order to clear. Mere words will not do it. Since it is buried within your body, as tension, your whole being, and especially your physical body, needs to express a buried or suppressed resentment. Words may suffice for a present resentment—you are already connected.

Put-downs and judgments do not clear effectively. It is important to use the "I am," not "you are" or "it is," to connect to low self at the clearing level. Put-downs and judgments are alienating. They go as if we were better than the other person, and our low self knows the end result of this. We have no right to put ourselves above one another, so put-downs and judgments may relieve pressure momentarily, but since they are creating something else which may require clearing, the end result may not be gained. They are, however, valuable for working into an emotional connection. And they can be used for this, provided that they are acknowledged for what they are. I give an imaginary card to those with whom I work. It says: THE RIGHT TO BE OUTRAGEOUS.

Admitting to outrageousness can allow spontaneity. Strangely, if we know and admit that it is outrageous to use these clearing tools, then even the person whose actions we are clearing will not be alienated. If they are present it is important to look at them and say, "this may be outrageous."

The next step after being "outrageous" is to clean it up by moving from the outrageous "you are" judgments and put-downs to the "I hate" mentioned above. It is important not to leave it at the outrageous if you want to feel really clear. Example: "You dirty low-down skunk! You no-good etc." can be cleaned up with the specifics of what action caused our anger, and then the clarity to say, "and I hate that."

Recognizing loaded expressions. It is important to recognize "loaded" where the weight of the feeling is heavy with uncleared feeling from similar situations, often with other people than the one with whom we are trying to clear now. If we recognize loadedness, we can say "This feels loaded;" or we can hope to have our friends recognize loadedness and communicate "that feels loaded." Being aware of loaded expression may help us understand how we are having difficulty clearing *this* specific.

Anger and hate are not the same. Anger and hate are not the same thing. To me they refer to the same emotion with a different time orientation. Anger is unexpressed, held-in hate. Hating is NOW: "I hate . . . NOW." When I say, "I am angry," this is "aboutism." I am *describing* me.

In *Human Behaviour,* April 1977, is an interview with Manfred Clynes, a concert-pianist-turned-neurophysiologist who believes he has discovered a scientific method for measuring and studying how we communicate emotions. When asked if some emotions are more difficult to get in touch with than others, he replied: "In our society, reverence and hate often cause difficulty in clear sentic expression. Many Americans, for one thing, simply aren't familiar with reverence. Once they discover it through sentics, however, it becomes very releasing for them. *As for hate, we confuse it with anger.* (My italics.) The Japanese, in contrast, have no trouble at all differentiating anger and hate when doing sentic circles. The Japanese, so familiar with the mechanics of haiku, know when they are in NOWNESS. Americans think when they say: "I am angry," or "It is so beautiful," that they are expressing a feeling. They do not recognize "aboutism." It takes time for Americans to learn when they are in the NOW.

When asked what sequence he preferred in working with emotions, Clynes said; "First anger and hate, which involves a relatively strong motor action. Then grief. It's a motor collapse, a letting go, without hope or help. Then you're ready for the positive, love."

My experience is that the negative emotions which require clearing float to the top. When they are cleared, love happens spontaneously. The sequence Clynes gives is the one I find working, organically. Always work with the uppermost emotion, but warily. Often a person will pull up a secondary emotion to avoid expressing the one on top. Listen, and you can tell by the way this secondary one doesn't want to connect. Don't push the person. Stop the work. Let the person know your fantasy of what is happening. You can trust the organism. It will push its top emotion up, given time and space.

The emotion on top may be grief but you will find anger close behind. Usually anger is on top but is being expressed with non clearing ego-defensive aboutisms and judgments and put-downs, the tools of anger, for anger usually wants to hurt someone. Transform this to hating which is pure clearing. Then may come grief. When anger, hate and grief are cleared, love happens. Magically. Try it.

Loving, hating, grieving and regretting are key emotions. They are very NOW. There are also STATES of emotion and these are frequently confused with emotion itself. States of emotion are related to aboutism and it is important to realize the difference and to move from the state (anger) to the emoting. Emoting! It is a happening. It is now. The state is something which can be described. Aboutism (I am angry) does not clear us.

Most of us, afraid of our emotions, or afraid of showing them, communicate the state, not the emotion. Often people who describe their states believe they are being real. They are not. If we are around them for long we get overloaded hearing about their states. We get bored. We do not get bored when someone emotes. *Move from the state into the emotion.* Try this: becoming aware of a state, move into emoting it without words, using only sounds and body movements, making a dance of it. If words come spontaneously, then allow them. Feel the difference.

From the interview mentioned with Clynes:

Q. You might intuitively expect disappointment or dejection to be composed of unhappiness and anger. (All of these are states.)

A. We have started working with compound feelings, things like melancholy and envy, yes. It's remarkable how the biologic system seems to communicate the essence of these qualities as mixtures. Your question points up the problems raised by words. How are you to differentiate between disappointment and dejection? Dictionaries are good for looking up words, but I don't look for truth in them.

The problems raised by words! "I feel that" for "it is my opinion that;" "I am angry" for "I hate (that)!" Roszak was aware of this when he said: "a generation that had grown dubious about the reliability of speech, and had already attuned itself to hearing the character behind . . . "[3] A generation, I see as I work with them, which knows there is something not to be trusted, but does not yet know the specific warning signs. And not knowing the signs, perpetuates the patterns with which they are uncomfortable.

In a *New Age* interview with the Simontons, Carl and Stephanie, who have been working together on a special project involving the emotional needs of cancer people, Carl says: " . . . emotional depression in reaction to stress seems to result in physical depression of the body's immune system . . . " Therefore " . . . curing cancer is not a question of killing all the cancer cells . . . but of causing a body to return to what it normally does."

It would seem that cancer patients need to discover more valid choices in their means of dealing with stress situations. Carl Simonton says that when we are sick may be a hard time to do that but "confronting belief systems in our minds can be a step toward changing belief systems." This fits with what I indicated previously, that not taking the right to hate prevents us from clearing our anger. And it also fits with what the Kahunas stress and what Seth stresses in *The Nature of Personal Reality*, that examining our belief system is a first step in dealing with emotional problems.

One of the things Stephanie Simonton has to say echoes very deeply with my experience with therapy: "Patients who expect to be miraculously healed by being in the same room with us are not likely to do well." Patients need to realize their responsibility to participate in the healing process.

3. Roszak, T. *The Making of a Counter Culture,* p. 191.

Their ability to try on new choices of behaviour is important to the healing process. Especially with anger. Carl Simonton says: "People prone to cancer tend to harbour resentments and hold in anger more. They are often labelled "do-gooders" because they are primarily concerned with pleasing others. At the same time they see themselves as victims . . . " And the children of this type of person have two strikes against them:

1. They see their parent (parents) as doing good rather than playing the martyr, which is what is really happening. Their right to hate what is happening is thwarted by this image (belief).

2. They have had holding back resentments, holding in anger, as their model of dealing with feelings. In this way they perpetuate cancer-producing patterns. They need to start by taking the right to hate. In order to do this they may first need to explore their belief systems.

EXERCISES

1. *BELIEFS*

Share with others some of the things you feel strongly about in connection with someone close to you. Apply it to a specific person. You may be surprised how being specific connects you more strongly to your feelings. Share with a partner some of your beliefs about:

(a) responsibility

(b) needs

(c) how to deal with discomforts in a relationship with someone with whom you live or work

Do the same with your beliefs about:

(d) the right to hate

(e) the right to cry

2. *CLEARING ANGER*

Choose someone in your life with whom you are angry or could be angry. Using the two-chair method—one for you, one for the imaginary other—switch to the other chair frequently to keep in touch with how you believe the other person would repond to your clearing. Notice when you are being judgmental or using putdowns and try switching these to "I hate (when you do . . .)" expressions. Feel the difference. See if you are communicating to the other person the specific time, place and happening with which you are uncomfortable.

3. *EXPRESSING GRIEF*

Work with grief in the same way, using the two-chair method, switching frequently. Share with the other person your memories, your feeling of loss, your regrets, your appreciations, and your resentments. Finish with appreciations.

It was an ancient rule of the Hawaiians that "no one should hurt another bodily, or through theft of goods, or through injury to feelings."
These were the only sins. . . .

—Max Freedom Long
The Secret Science Behind Miracles, p. 281

3

POWERLESSNESS AND AGGRESSION

We have a right to every one of our feelings; we do not have the right to hurt someone with them. We have the right to hate as much as we have the right to love. Many children have been robbed of their rights to feelings, through non-hearing or rationalization of them, when what they needed was to be shown how to express their feelings without hurting someone with them.

A child who has been robbed of the right to feelings, or has not learned valid ways of clearing them will end up hurting, self or others. As a result the low self will, at a deep level, feel invalid, without force or foundation, unable to contact High Self.

Following are some of the theories which I have developed over the years, as I have observed what happens in groups and in communal living situations:

Theory 1: That *clearing* resentments results in our being more loving.

Theory 2: That "holding in" resentments results in body tensions that:
- (a) stop our energy flow and lead to serious illness
- (b) result in isolation and depression.

Theory 3: That held-in resentments are covertly expressed in hurtful ways.

Outwardly

By complaining
By gossiping
By put-downs—sarcasm, criticism, labelling or name-calling
By acting helpless, sucking energy from people around us, draining others with our bottomless well of needs
By being destructive. I once had a mechanic tell me that he had noticed that people with held-in resentments would likely be rough on their cars. I have known people with strong held-in anger who had poltergeist effects wherever they lived.

Inwardly

By putting ourselves down
By pushing ourselves; i.e., to be successful.
By turning our resentments in on ourselves, being self-destructive. An example would be if we feel like choking someone we choke up; if we feel like killing someone, we kill ourselves (suicide).

In all of these ways we hurt self or other.

That our society tends to be invasive (hurtful) of others reflects in our language: Aggression appears to be a prized quality today: "He is an aggressive salesman."

I have seen encounter groups encourage aggression; I believe those leaders are confusing aggression and assertiveness. In a dictionary I have assertion is given as insistence on a right and aggression is given as unprovoked attack. Yet it seems aggression, "unprovoked attack," has become a positive value to some segments of our society. Somewhere we have lost touch with the hurt involved in aggression. I believe this can be traced in part to our having lost both the rights to our feelings and the awareness of what we do with them.

Clynes, in the interview I mentioned with *Human Behavior*, said that "learning to express (emotions) seems to take away from the human drive toward violence."

Over the years I have become aware of three places of power or lack of it which are quite easy to recognize, and awareness of them can facilitate working with "complexes." I take as my example the university drop-outs of the 60's: most students were acquiescing to the pressures of the "big machine," as I call the authoritarian campus. Then came the rebels, and finally the drop-outs who are forming now alternatives of their own.

First there was helplessness, where the students felt they had few rights in their own lives, but were controlled by the authorities. Next there was rebellion. This is still a powerless state: the authority has the power. In this state we are rebelling against the authority and needing it at the same time. We try, first, to convince "the power" of our rights, of our discomforts. Then, if we are not "heard" we rebel. Rebels put a lot of energy into getting others on their side so that they may prevail against the authority. They are lively. They criticize. They push. They judge. But in reality the rebel is still in a powerless spot. The "other" still has the power. The third place is usually a rough one since it appears the "other" still has the resources, and we have to start from scratch. But we choose to do so, taking back the power in our lives, "giving ourselves up to life," as Seth puts it, with whatever resources we have.

This pattern of HELPLESSNESS-REBELLION-SELF-ACTUALIZATION can be found in individual lives, and it is important for me to notice which one is operating, both in myself and in others. It took me a while to recognize that the rebel is not coming from a place of power. I was thrown off by the rebel's strong voice, by the rebel's aliveness. We are not free if we need to rebel. Neither is the authority free when power must be imposed. Only when authority is given is it free.

This indicates a subtle interplay between power and freedom. The people at Findhorn understand this very well. Here there are authorities, in the sense of wisdom, not of control. Their authority has been given by their contemporaries. Changes at Findhorn take place organically. And power is not imposed; it comes from organic unity, which is a subtle ever-changing process. The people who go there are there for the experience.

In contrast, most students at the big-machine universities are there for their degrees. They are not committed so much to the process as they are to the end result, the degree. And the authorities control the process through the end result. I was surprised when I met Fritz Perls, that he did not ask for my degree standing. His questions were more subtle, finding out where I was with myself, and with group process. Fritz taught us to trust the organism. That is the way he worked at Cowichan. The only diploma I ever heard of Fritz giving was one to a fellow trainee, a piece of toilet paper with the words: Irwin can now wipe his own ass.

I thank both Findhorn and Cowichan for teaching me that time schedule and structure are part of the process which allows the organism to work freely, but that these are only valid when they are determined by the community as a whole, changeable by that community as the community feels need for change.

Most of us are still operating in a world of controls, not realizing there is, in our lives, the possibility of organic process, individually as well as communally. So long as we operate in a world of controls we become adept at manipulating. At university the authority might manipulate by forcing materials and methods which are irrelevant to the student, giving grades only for this material. The rebel might manipulate by attempting to disrupt the program in order to be heard, the helpless one by cheating.

In taking back our power we need to be aware of the place

from which we are starting, the helpless one or the rebel. Don't be fooled by the rebel. Appreciate his/her liveness but realize there is work to do. I believe the rebel is one stage ahead of the helpless one who doesn't even grasp the possibility of freedom. I find it unreal to expect someone to move directly from helplessness to stength. So often we need our rebel for a while.

THE HELPLESS ONE is, in reality, manipulative:

Tries to get sympathy, plays the martyr
—Look what the world is (you are) doing to me.
—Look what I've done for you.
—I'll make you feel guilty.

Complains
—The world's not right.
—You change it for me.

Uses aboutism constantly; gossips, not making contact with the situation.
—Without risk I'll get your sympathy on my side.

Uses generalities like "never" and "always"
—It's always hopeless.
—It never changes.

Drones on and on, or shuts off completely
—I'll get your attention (energy) one way or another.

That is the organism taking care of itself the best way it knows how, only its choices are very limited. The results can be destructive, especially to children who have helpless parents.

THE REBEL

Shouts. Lets you know they are here.

Condemns the authority. Uses judgments and put-downs.

Demands. Expects the authority to meet these demands whether they are agreeable to the authority or not.

Wants to hurt. Is destructive or disrespectful of the authority, property, feelings, etc.

Tries to get others on his/her side, in order to control or decimate the "authority."

The more powerless we feel the more we act the part of the victim. We can't tell what to do, we can't enjoy ourselves, we don't know how to deal with the world. The rebel at least is trying. What the rebel needs is to give up the authority's "carrot," whatever that may be, and to live for him/herself, with whatever resources he/she has. The helpless one needs to look at rights, especially the right to feelings. The more powerless we feel, the more potential for hurting others.

To the Hunas, "hurting" is extremely important. Max Freedom Long says:

> *In Huna there is one great sin which can be consciously committed, and only one: that of HURTING ANOTHER.*

He says successful connection with High Self canot be made while one feels guilty of hurting others. Where the Kahuna (healer) starts is with clearing these trespasses, and the "complexes" or fixations which cause them—and then making choices.

Sounds reminiscent of the NLP method in the first chapter.

Going back to theory 3 in this chapter in hurtful ways that held-in resenments are covertly expressed, I believe that to get to our "High Self" power it is more important to find valid choices of dealing with our discomforts than it is to continue to rebel, or to be manipulatively helpless. And there is the way I gave in Chapter 1, of moving from aboutism to NOW communication, taking first the right to our feelings, and then honoring these feelings in the best way we know how, without draining or aggressive others, expressing our feelings clearly and cleanly, trusting that this works organically, by itself, simply letting others know. I love this. I hate that. If we are heard it's beautiful. If not, we go where hearing may happen, living in such a way that we do not rob others of their freedom to give or not to give the responses we think we need.

This third is the way of personal power, of depending on our own resources, trusting the organism of the universe.

To state our needs without being attached to having specific persons fill them for us, is to allow some of our friends the joy of giving, rather than giving out of being expected to. There is quite a difference.

Exercises

1. *GESTALT WRESTLING.* So that no one will be hurt, use a soft mat and make sure that each of the two wrestlers stays on his/her knees throughout the "match," unless they are toppled over. Otherwise the rules for "pinning" are the same as in ordinary wrestling: a win is declared when both of the opponent's shoulders are "pinned" simultaneously. There must be no harmful holds.

Since frequently one partner is bigger than, or stronger than the other, in this wrestling there are two rounds. For the second round the one who was pinned in the first one gets to pin the other in the second round. Only this time the one who did the pinning the first time allows him/herself to be pinned, but *only* when he/she feels the other giving their limit of trying, their full assertiveness.

Particularly notice which one is operating at various points: your helpless-one, your rebel, or your fully into it, assertive self. After the match allow "play-back" from the others.

2. Take turns telling someone some things you want. Now switch and say "I need—" for the same things. Feel the difference, if there is any.

Do the same with, "I have to—" switching to "I choose to—." Do the same with "I can't—" switching to "I won't—."

3. Take a situation where you are not getting something you want/need from someone. Using the two-chair method imagine yourself having a conversation about it, with them, switching places frequently, playing both parts. Notice particularly with what the other feels uncomfortable and how they communicate this.

Get playback after you are finished: Did the others experience your helpless-one or your rebel? When and how? How could you have become more centred? What are your alternative choices? Experiment until you find what feels good to you. You have more choices than you realize. Perhaps you are trying to have your cake and eat it too. Watch out for that one.

4. For a clearer understanding of the relation between powerlessness and aggression read *Why Men Rape* (which consists of interviews with convicted rapists), edited by Sylvia Levine and Joseph King.

Western culture has basically emphasized the head centre. That is why in the West a deep concern is felt for man. And the deep concern is with his homelessness, his emptiness. . . . The reason is because only the head has become center. The heart has not been trained; it is missing.

—Rajneesh
The Book of Secrets, p. 215

4

THE HOLE OR BOTTOMLESS WELL
in Huna—the "Complex"

Now I want to talk about the "missing potential," the "hole" as Fritz Perls called it, the bottomless well of need. Another way of describing the missing potential might be to say powerlessness. Symptoms of holes are avoidances. When we get close to the impasse we get confused. The impasse is the point where we believe we have no choice, no power in our lives. Whatever the choice, it would involve too much risk for us. We try to find an easier way, our low self all the while aware that this easier way doesn't do it, doesn't connect with the High Self. We are stuck.

The impasse, signalled by confusion, or by deadness if we have completely given up, is *where* we are stuck. Now it is important to find out *how*. Usually we are looking for someone to solve our problems for us, and no-one is willing. We give our power, in that way, to others. We believe we ourselves are powerless in this situation. Stay with the impasse and discover this "how." What is it we are not capable of supplying for ourselves? What is our hole? What are we afraid of? Whatever it is, our hole represents something we believe we need; it may be some support we needed, at some specific time long ago, a basic need which did not get filled. And we are stuck with the pain of the emptiness. We are still trying to get it, from someone, even though it may be something we could now deal with ourselves. We are still living as if we are powerless, or not worth while. Whether we are working with the hole in a present situation or a past one is relative; we need to be there, now, experiencing or re-experiencing our need, discovering *our* potential to deal with it, NOW.

Breathing, gestures, voice, body tensions, emotions will give clues whether we are in a weak spot or have moved to a strong one. Become aware of these signals as you move through pain into freedom from pain; from need of support to self-support. We need to go into the pain to know it, to discover how we might move through it. Not going through it, we prolong the world of pain. If our signals show complaint of helplessness, what might change that? What demand do we need to make into the past? What need to express? And to whom? The risk we avoid taking is that of facing the pain, the hopelessness, which could bring our freedom, through taking the right to express our needs, without attachment to them. No other can do this for us. But there is reward. To discover our potential to come through the pain and find ourselves still here is a rebirth.

Be aware of the difference between wants and needs. Abraham Maslow gave us excellent guidelines here with his hierarchy of needs: physical nourishment, safety, love, esteem and self-actualization, in that order. Self-actualization is that stage at which we have the maturity to "become" authentically, moment by moment, or, as Fritz would put it, to have response-ability, moment by moment.

Self-actualization happens at the stage when we are no longer bound by anxiety but are aware of the phoniness of our head trips and aboutisms, when these are not at one with our hearts; when we acknowledge the phoniness of our "split" responses, yet have the ability to live, authentically with this knowlege, because in recognizing the difference between "center" and "split" we know where our work lies. It is a trusting of our potential, having the maturity to experience, not to avoid, our unreality. Self-actualization comes at the point when truth sets us free to make a choice, the point when we are responding, not re-acting.

Until self-actualization, our perceptions are colored by our need to "have." In order to perceive "beingly" it is first necessary to experience "having" needs sufficiently met, or of being willing to take the risk of dying to these needs. Anxiety prevents the experience of self-actualization. Hang-ups at any level lead to decay. At the self-actualization point we cannot escape death, either the decay of being stuck frozen, or a psychic death which allows egocentric anxiety perceptions to be supplanted by willingness to take a risk.

When a person or civilization has its basic needs met it is as natural to move into the next phase as it is for a flower to bloom: there is a strong instinctive urge to move. When that urge is thwarted by a hang-up or anxiety about a past need there is neurosis—a stuckness. Then, only a knowing or facing the anxiety can constructively relax the tension; the alternative is decay. Neurosis is the symptom which lets us know it is time to discover what is causing the hang-up. Neurosis is natural because it warns us against decay. It is trying to let us know that what we can be must be. It is part of the organic process.

In the organic process the basic need is for physical nourishment. If this need is not met we would die. If this is satisfied, then safety is our next need. I know a number of Jewish people who are, even in 1980, living in anxiety because of the treatment their relatives received at the hands of the Germans in the Second World War. When a need for safety has not been met it has remained as a hole affecting even their children who were born after the war.

In America it seems our holes are more related to love and esteem, connected to the urge to achieve (future), which puts feelings secondary, or turns a deaf ear. Our hole disappears to the extent we take a right to our feelings and our own beliefs.

Another impasse place is related to imposed values. If my right and wrong, good and bad, come from me, I can become centered by checking with my heart (low self). But if my values are imposed on me, or "swallowed," without ever having been checked with my heart, then I may still remain split. I may be going this path with my head while my heart wants to go elsewhere. There is no way we can go opposite paths at the same time, so what results is an impasse.

If I have not learned to listen to my heart (low self), then this part, connected to my needs, is missing from my awareness, and I wonder what is wrong. This disconnection from my feeling center may have happened when I was very young. I may have had so much value system imposed on me that I do not realize I have a right to check with my heart. Even if I did believe I had a right I may not know how to do so.

Certainly children have to develop trust in checking with their hearts as middle self values come into their lives, and a wise parent sees that they have as much opportunity as possible to do so. The more they develop this faculty the more centered they will be. For those who had not developed this faculty, Fritz Perls originated in therapy the two-chair method for integration, putting underdog (low self) on one chair and topdog (middle self) on the other. It is a valuable exercise for anyone and particularly for those who were denied or not encouraged in its use as a child.

Where some of the difficulty comes with parents, and indeed with all of us, is in not understanding the difference between wants and needs. *The needs listed by Maslow in his hierarchy are "growing needs." When these are not met in their organic or natural progression, then they become the holes I mentioned, and they turn into wants:* I want something to fill that hole. We go around, sometimes desperately, trying one thing after another, yet never finding more than temporary satisfaction; we need to go down into the hole, ourselves.

It is important in working with holes to feel the difference between wants and needs, and to help children to understand the difference. We need to be aware that when a child says "I want" he/she may be signalling a hole that needs attention, some "growing" need that is not being met. I have seen a little boy "bug" his mother incessantly with wants, which she dutifully tried to sort out but which were "driving her off her rocker" because she was engrossed in heavy problems of her own. What I noticed was that she was so distracted she answered him but seldom made contact. She heard him, at times, in the physical sense, but not in the heart to heart, hearing sense. And what I became aware of was that his need was for this real contact, not for his wants. She understood what I meant by contact, and when she gave him this, an amazing thing happened: minutes of contact resulted in hours of non-bugging. How very little he needed to be self-sufficient and non-draining!

Our needs and wants get more complex as we get older and more disconnected from the source of our unfilled needs. Then we want all sorts of things to fill our bottomless wells. I call them bottomless because none of our feelings really work. We are satisfied temporarily, but the need still drives us. And our using of others to fill our holes results in isolation from them, which makes us more hopeless. What is required is to discover the original need by going into the hole, and to deal with that. Do it through the emotions, with the feeling connected to the hole. Making sounds along with body movements can be very effective to get connected, but we must be completely into the feeling, expressing it, to know it and to go through it. Try getting into some bioenergetic groups for some guidance in how to do this. There are people who can hear when you are connected and to what emotion; they can see, hear, or feel your physical blocks, and can give you appropriate exercises.

Rolfing and rebirthing are methods you might try. I believe that many people use sex to try to fill their hole (and there's a meaningful pun here). If we are doing this, our hole may be signalled by our partner feeling used, or the relationship being unsatisfying to us. Bottomless wells can't be filled with wants, although for sure we will try, especially with something as attractive to us as sex. Only when we distinguish the need-turned-into-want and are able to go down into the well and deal with it ourselves will we be free, for the organism is driving us to completion of the unfinished gestalt.

You will recognize the bottomless-well want by noticing how those things you believed you needed to dispel this emptiness do not work. Then you could look for ways of discovering your own potential to deal with those needs.

Seth, in *The Nature of Personal Reality*, p. 31, says, "You chose your environment. It carries the challenges you need to work out your own reality."

Some suggestions in this chapter and at the end of it may be of use to you in doing so.

Exercises

1. *SHARING:* (group)

Tell a partner a current big need and say what you have done about it, and what you plan to try. After each pair has completed sharing in this way the group forms a circle. Each partner of the pairs becomes an advocate for the other, sharing with the group what they have understood of the need and what is being done about it. Then have the group explore where the need fits in Maslow's hierarchy: food, safety, love, esteem, self-actualization.

2. *CHOICE:* (group)

Tell the others something you feel you have to do then change and say "I choose to—" to the same thing. Feel the difference.

3. *ESTEEM:* (group or singly)

Remember a situation where you felt unappreciated and experienced a need for esteem. Now picture a situation where you felt none of this need. What were the ingredients in the second situation which left you free? How would you get these ingredients into the first situation?

4. *POWER:* (group, sitting)

Picture to the group a situation in your life where you would like to say "No" or "I won't" or "Stop."

Stand and say the words or word and let the group mirror whether you sound connected to your power spot or not. They respond, as they experience you, by

—staying put if no power
—rising slightly according to the power they experience from you
—standing when they hear you come from centre

Repeat the same word and keep trying, until you feel satisfied, or until everyone is standing.

5. *MY HEART'S NOT INTO IT:* (group or single)

Find out if "My heart's not into it." or "My heart's into it." about some of the choices you are making in your life right now.

What are some of the things your heart's not into NOW?

Explore how you are dealing with these.

Do the same with things your heart is into doing, but which you are not doing now.

6. *RIGHT-TO-DO-NOTHING DAY:* (single)

Once in a while take a right-to-do-nothing day. This does not mean you must do nothing. That would be having to do something. A right-to-do-nothing day allows you to do only what your heart is into. There is nothing in this day that you *have* to do.

And you can hear it [whatsoever is given] between the words, you can read it between the lines—then words are just an excuse. The real thing happens just by the side of the words.

—Rajneesh
Only One Sky, p. 9

5

COMMUNICATION

For me the most powerful measure of how effective our communication is likely to be, is how we express our feelings. And how we express them depends on:

1. Our ability to own our beliefs as personal; to take the right to them as such. Our ability to say I believe or I don't believe without rationalizing, without building a case for our beliefs, yet being aware of how we got them. Our ability to allow equal rights of others to their beliefs, aware that these also are personal, not to be reacted to, but to be received as communication of that person.

2. The validity for each of us of the whole spectrum of feelings, from hate to love, from resentment to appreciation, from sadness to joy, from discomfort to comfort, and our ability to communicate and receive these feelings as interaction, not re-action.

3. Our ability to distinguish nowness from aboutism; our ability to know when we are connected to low self, expressing out of our feelings (coming from center), rather than from head trips (rationalizations).

4. Our ability to *express* our feelings as a communication, a giving, of ourselves; not using their power for accusation,

or as a dagger, to destroy, to hurt, or, in the case of "wanty" love, to swallow, to limit another.

5. Our ability to clear and to stay clear, to recognize when we are coming on loaded, and to have tools to unload or detonate safely.
6. Our ability to know when we are heard and not heard, and our ability to listen.
7. Our trust of center, our freedom from defensiveness, our response-ability.

Is our communication damaging or healing?

I believe that most of our hurts happen in everyday communication—communication in our homes—and that it is out of this stuff that wars are made. This chapter is concerned with warning signals which we can use to discover when and how communication breaks down; and to give some suggestions which may help in achieving healthy rather than harmful communication.

In "groups" we have a daily resentment-appreciation time, clearing anything unexpressed of either. Appreciations are usually welcomed in whatever form we give them, even judgmental ones such as "You did a good job—." Not so resentments: "You did a bad job—." This is likely to bring up defensiveness or non-hearing. And hearing is essential to clearing. Hearing does not promise I will change, but rather that what I have heard will be part of my interaction with that person.

How often do we go on and on, filling the air with words, all of which enter the others' ears,—but are not heard! Even worse, the wall between us gets thicker and thicker, the distance greater, because, on one side, of the defences needed against this useless and endless barrage of words; and on the other side, of the feeling of being unheard. Although we know the wall is getting thicker we do not understand how we are creating it. The problem lies in *how* we communicate our discomforts, our resentments, our needs. In the following I will give some of the patterns which do *not* work towards effective communication. Listen for them, and if you are using them in your communication, try the accompanying suggestions for "clearing."

Authoritarian Judgments, Fact-Giving and Opinions

Signalled by sentences beginning, "It is—," "You are—," "They should—," etc.

Putting ourselves above others in this way, as an authority, seems to make us feel in control, or on top of things. In fact we may be using aboutism to try to make contact, while at the same time we are keeping ourselves distant with aboutism. A similar pattern is exhibited by the person who, as a means of contact, is continually giving facts or advice. These are potentially deadening patterns. As part of the organic process, the low self of the other, at some point, automatically shuts off.

a. The hearer can notice when he/she feels tired of listening and can say so: "I'm tired of listening. I would like to be quiet for a while."

b. Often there is more contact in silence than in the talking about times. Experiment by agreeing on a silent (nonverbal) day once in a while.

c. Authoritarians can start to change patterns of aboutism by beginning to express feelings, what they appreciate or resent; what they are comfortable or uncomfortable with, keeping it simple, "I resent (or appreciate)—." With no explanations, just stating what they resent or appreciate. Beware of talking about your feelings as opposed to expressing them. You may need to start with "I am angry" (description), but practice moving into *expressing,* with your whole body, your voice, your actions. Use the strong phrases "I hate—," "I love—," "I need—," "I believe—," to get connected. When you notice yourself using an opinion or judgment, switch to an "I hate that" and give specifics.

Instead of "It is—" kinds of statements, try saying, "I believe it is—," letting yourself connect more. Don't build cases for either feelings or "heart" beliefs. Unlike opinions, neither of them requires this. They stand on their own as a statement of us. A belief has more validity than an opinion; it may even have the same validity as a feeling; it is certainly as powerful. Our feelings come from our beliefs; we can trust our feelings to be true, not always our beliefs. Just as feelings are expressed with "I—" sentences, so are beliefs: "I believe—." One "you" statement has, perhaps, the same validity as an "I—" statement; it is "You have no right to—." When we talk about rights, beliefs are implicit.

Rationalizing or "building a case" will not clear resentments. It is probably one of the most time-consuming, energy-depleting, ineffective ways of attempting to do so. It leads to taking sides, one-upmanship, endless arguments, recriminations and opinions.

Move from aboutism to communication (See chapter 1 and the exercises at the end of this chapter for how). This needs to be done early, before the energy to express a feeling becomes too wasted.

Manipulative Why's

One of the most powerful blocks to the expression of feelings, particularly those of children, is manipulative WHY: "Why did you do that?"

Why immediately makes the communication into an argument, a head trip. It is subtly intended to make the other answer to us whether we are aware of this or not. It is a pin-down device, which says, in effect, "You come to me instead of me exposing myself to you. Then I can stay in control."

One of Fritz Perls' most effective ways of dealing with manipulative "Why's" was to say, "Make a statement out of that." And once, with someone who knew about manipulative "why's," I saw Fritz deliberately not answer yet very obviously stay in contact, until the person caught on and changed "why" into a statement. Fritz would not get sucked into a manipulative "why." Try spotting manipulative "why's" of your own as well as those of others, and changing them to statements. "Why did you do that?" might translate, "I resent when you do that."

When another uses a manipulative why, ask them to make that into a statement.

Spot the Phony "I Feel That"

Which is not a feeling, but an evasion of feeling, used, again, to try to keep "on top of things." It is a subconscious attempt to get the validity of a feeling for an opinion or a belief.

It may be either an opinion or a belief. That is what you need to check. If it is an opinion take the responsibility of saying so. If it is a belief, take the risk of saying "I believe" instead of "I feel that."

Name-Calling or Labeling

I see these also as subtle put-downs and attempts to stay above things, rather than giving clear statements of what is being felt. For me they are a signal of powerlessness in the person using them.

Try making a clear statement: "I believe," not "You stupid ass."

> *Because we are starting from a weak place with our rebel or our helpless one we may need to use the tools of these places in order to connect. For that, they are valuable. But make the switch to "I am" statements and after a while you will begin to come from there. Don't get stuck in name-calling.*

Fuzziness and Generality do not help to clear a feeling; every resentment comes from a specific happening, at a specific time and place, a NOW. Generality is related to aboutism; it is not here and now; it is not experiential. And feeling, to be expressed, must come out of experience; it must be connected to specific happening.

> *The one who is expressing the resentment may be fuzzy himself about how the resentment happened. Move from the fuzzy to the specific of time, place, and action.* Discover the exact time when the discomfort set in *and how it happened.*

> *Don't bring a resentment off a generality: "I hate your selfishness." What is selfishness for one may not be for another. Say what* you *experienced as selfishness, and then you can say "and I hate that, it looks selfish to me."*

> Nor off a judgment: *"I hate your being selfish" also has judgment in it. Clear your statement with time, place, and action, allowing others their own judgment. This does not stop you from having the feeling of resentment towards the act. And it helps you to communicate it so that others have freedom to judge for themselves.*

Bringing a Resentment off a Fantasy

By fantasy I mean my own private view of how things are with someone or something other than myself, what I imagine are someone else's motives and feelings. Often we take our fantasies as fact and our resentments come off imaginations which are untrue. If this is the case the clearing will miss the mark.

Checking fantasies is very important. If the hearer senses something not fitting, check for fantasy.

Exercises

MONOPOLIZATION, NON-LISTENING

Usually this comes from a need for ego-building or from building a case for a feeling, instead of trying to clarify the time, place and "how" mentioned above.

The signal will be that the hearer will feel bogged down with a lot of talking. Be aware, and deal with this. A resentment requires only one clear sentence, to say time, place, and happening related to the feeling. It is haiku-like. And the silence, afterward, will encourage more hearing than all the case building ever could. A feeling does not require a case to be built for it; it stands on its own.

LOADEDNESS: which I dealt with in chapter 2.

If you are feeling loaded with past resentments; or if the hearer senses loading:

Step 1—Say "I feel loaded," or "This may not all be for you." If the hearer picks up loadedness the hearer can let you know. "That sounds loaded to me."

Step 2—Pretend that the person with whom you are trying to clear, presently, is sitting on an empty chair, and give them all you are feeling without sorting out which is loaded. Do not give loadedness *directly* to the person. Then feel how much of what you cleared is for them. When you are clearing loadedness in this way take your "outrageous" ticket and let go—judgments, name-calling, stamping on the floor, hitting a pillow, wringing a towel, biting a towel, whatever feels good, until you are connected.

Step 3—Come to the point where you can say, clearly, "and I hate *that*." Notice how this cleans up any judgments or put-downs. You will feel the difference. Watch for it. Use it frequently. It helps you keep clear as you "work."

Very often, when working with loadedness, resentments towards others will replace those towards the person with whom you started. Let them happen, with whatever force they have, until they are clear. Then go back to the person with whom you started, checking whether you are finished with them, also. If you are, you will have demolished a wall between you, and both of you will be aware of it.

Even children feel safer when you get your loadedness out using the empty chair method; even children are aware of the air's being clearer, providing you clean up your put-downs with "I hate (specifics). They can feel the difference and they will appreciate it. It is good to explain to them, first, what you are doing—that you are unloading, and it isn't meant for them to take it on.

Sometimes I clear loadedness when I am driving alone. Only I make sure I am in a safe place, where I can slow down (very slow), or stop my car. You don't need the "other chair," but if the one whom you are giving the loaded resentment to is present, using the other chair helps to let them know the loadedness is not being pushed at them.

Complaining comes from a weak place and causes non-hearing, and resentment in return. Complaining has no end, it goes on and on, never being satisfied, and in this way it is alienating.

For the complainer:

Move from complaining, every time you become aware of it, to "I hate—," or "I resent—," or "I need," statements, and then let go. Make the statements as short as you can, only long enough to give specifics. The shorter the better.

For the hearer:

Simply say "I hear complaining," letting the other know you are not interested in listening to that form of communication. Often complaining is more of the voice than of words.

Gossiping is related to complaining. I tell the gossiper to tell it to the person concerned; I am not interested in gossip.

Whenever we hear gossiping or complaining in our community, that is a signal for us to have a resentment-appreciation meeting to clear things up.

Related to complaining is

Laying a Guilt Trip or Playing the "Martyr"

This comes from helplessness, from an inability to express feelings cleanly, or even from unawareness of the feelings themselves, and consequently wanting others to fill our bottomless well of need. These are manipulations, subconsciously intended to make the other feel guilty enough that we can get from them what we want. The one who lays these trips will not likely believe they are doing that. It is up to the other to recognize guilt trips and not take them on. For both the guilt-tripper and the martyr, throw others on their own resources. You don't help them by getting sucked into their trips. Let them know you are hearing a martyr by saying "I'm hearing a martyr!"

1. *Try saying "I need—" to them whenever you need something from someone else. Then discover whether you are free to "let go" of the expectation for them to fill it. It is important* both *to say your need, and to let go of the ex-*

pectation that others fill it for you. The filling of your need then comes as a gift, if it happens. Expectation deadens the joy of giving and receiving.

2. *See the exercises at the end of the Power-guilt chapter.*

Accusation

Beware of starting a sentence with a "pointed finger" "You—." "You haven't done the dishes yet."

Accusation, implying they should have. Notice this invites excuses or defensiveness.

Try changing the communication to an "I am—" one: "I'm pissed off that you haven't done the dishes yet." A simple statement of my feelings, not talking-down to the other, not pointing my finger, and not swallowing my resentment.

The Dagger

Used most often by the "rebel." The noise of the "rebel" will be heard, but the communication will not likely be "heard." It will literally feel like a dagger.

Let the other person know: That feels like a dagger.

Defensiveness

Signalled by excuses, is a sign of non-hearing. *The clean expression of a resentment requires no play-back—only hearing.*

If someone answers too quickly to have heard what you said, or if they answer with an excuse (defensiveness), one of two things is probably happening:

1. *The resentment was not given clearly; one of the destructive patterns above was likely happening, i.e., accusation. Then you would say "I feel accused."*

   OR

2. *The hearer may habitually be defensive, hearing clean resentment as accusation or judgment, etc. This would be*

loadedness from the hearer's past, and is very destructive to communication. Go no further until you clear up which is happening, and until the resentment is given clearly, and heard. If you feel your "hearer" is being defensive, say "I hear defensiveness." Anything else would be a waste of time.

Roszak, in *The Making of a Counter Culture*, speaks of organism and environment in a constant natural dialogue, an ongoing series of creative adjustments which make man at home in his body, his community, his natural habitat, and he says that neurosis sets in only when the seamless garment of the organism/environment field is divided by a psychic factionalism that segregates from the ecological whole a unit of defensive consciousness.

Most defensiveness signalled by non-hearing can be traced, I am sure, to one of the above-discussed patterns of communication, whether now or in the past.

Resentments, cleanly expressed, can lead to love. If you find this hard to believe, that anyone can welcome the communication of a resentment, then picture yourself living with someone who does not express their resentments. Do you believe you will not be experiencing them in some form? Resentments, uncleared, are there like a wall between you. If the other is not able to communicate the resentment, cleanly and specifically, you will feel mistrust. If their resentments build, you will feel as if you are living with a walking bomb; if their resentments are deadened, you will feel as if you are living with a plaster cast of a person. If the other gives their resentments in the harmful forms I have been dealing with above, you will feel uncomfortable.

Unless you have the maturity to deal with resentments in a way in which they can be cleared, love will have difficulty getting through. As cream floats on top of milk, so also do resentments stay on top. The first step in loving is to clear resentments out of the way; then love automatically happens. The above suggestions may help. They need practice, as music does, unless you already "play by ear."

Communication Practice

Learning to communicate more effectively can best be done in practice groups; one does not play, out in public, until one has practiced one's musical instrument sufficiently, or until one has first had a "safe" place to be "outrageous."

Frequently, people who have kept themselves squashed down, find so much joy in their first group clearing that they seem to want to catch up on all their lost childhood at once; however, they have not yet learned how to express their feelings cleanly. And their first attempts may backfire outside of groups. They may only be letting off steam, not clearing.

One man, especially, I remember, who lived in a communal house. And word came back to me that every time he got the least "pissed off" he went around slamming doors as hard as he could, letting all his loadedness reverberate through the house. Fortunately for him, his housemates understood what was happening and worked it out with him. It takes sensitivity on the part of others to be around the growth process. And that is part of the value of groups. They allow you to be outrageous while you are learning to connect to your feelings. You can form your own group.

I recommend you gather together a small group of friends for this purpose, and meet regularly, perhaps once a week, or for a week-end once a month. Or you can have a resentment-appreciation time in your own home, using the tools I have outlined in this chapter.

After each session re-read this chapter to understand more clearly what might have happened to gum things up, or just what happened to make you feel uncomfortable with someone. At the next session start with some sharing about it, staying with specifics and away from opinions and judgments. Just find out *when and how* the discomfort started, not why.

"Through adversity to the stars" the Canadian Air Force motto translates. That is something like groups. It isn't easy.

Welcome to the agony of change. If there is a hurt, cop to it. A hurt, acknowledged, is no longer a hurt, but can be a learning experience. A hurt, not acknowledged, can do much harm. One thing is certain: if hurting patterns are happening they will happen, anyway, somewhere. This way you have a chance to move beyond hurting, to love.

So form your own group. Allow yourselves the space to be "outrageous," compassionately. I suggest your group work with this book, one chapter at a time, in the order they are written.

You form the fabric of your experience through your own beliefs and expectation. . . . You take your beliefs about reality as truth, and often do not question them.

—Jane Roberts
The Nature of Personal Reality, p. 17

6

FANTASY

Fantasy is the forming of a mental image in our imagination of that which is "not me." All of us have fantasies; they are our private view of the world. Our problems come when we take them as someone else's reality. And when it has to do with their feelings toward us, this can become paranoia. Then our interaction, based on unreality, becomes unreal. At this point we need a way to discover reality.

The best way is to let the other person (persons) know we are having a fantasy of them we need to check. Since most people understand about fantasy they are usually quite willing to play back their "true" or "not-true." Whether we accept their answers as truth is something we have to work out for ourselves, exploring how their answers check with our experience of them. But at least it is in the open, being checked. If we do not give them our fantasy in the first place, the possibility of checking does not exist; but the possibility does exist of communicating with them in an unreal way.

Where fantasy can do most harm is in expression of negative feelings (anger, hate, resentment). We may be feeling resentment based on a fantasy that is not true; for instance, that people have no respect for private property, while in reality they had believed this was public property. Our resentment would miss the mark, since they may have a great deal of respect for private property. This exchange, then, would lead only to misunderstanding and mistrust, leaving uncomfortable, unresolved feelings unless someone caught on to what was happening, and even then there might be resentment that the person had not first checked their fantasy.

Beware of forming a resentment from either a judgment or a fantasy; it won't clear unless the judgment or fantasy fits the other person's reality. Checking fantasy has positive communication value.

The exercises given with this chapter may help you discover that.

Exercises

1. Give others our fantasies of:

   —what is important to them—of what is annoying to them
   —what they appreciate about us
   —what they have resented about us
   —what they mistrust
   —what they trust

   Have them play back their true or not true.

   This exercise is valuable between parents and children, husbands and wives, business partners, anyone with whom we have frequent contact. We fantasize that our parents' remembrance of past incidents is much the same as ours. Recall a particularly heavy time in your past where they were present. Recount it to your parents just as memory, without blame or judgment, just your feelings as you remember them. Check this with their remembrance of the incident.

Have them do the same with you. Notice whether these exercises improve your communication.

They (the kahunas) first took care that they had cleansed the patient of any sense of guilt left in the low self.

In Huna there is one great sin which can be consciously committed, and only one: that of HURTING ANOTHER.

—Max Freedom Long
The Secret Science at Work, p. 91

7

THE RELATION BETWEEN POWER AND GUILT

"Our concepts of 'sin' must be changed from all the customary beliefs and made to rest on one test alone. DOES THE ACT CAUSE AN INDIVIDUAL TO BE CUT OFF BY HIS LOW SELF FROM THE HIGH SELF?"[4]

When we are not connected to High Self we are not whole; we have lost touch with our higher power, our creativity, our greater insights, our source of growth.

The kahunas believed in, and performed their miracles through contact with the third and highest form of consciousness in man—that which we call for convenience, the High Self. It, like the low self and middle self is a spirit. It dwells in aka body outside the physical body. It may be close, or off at a distance, the aka cord always connects the low self and the High Self after the fashion of a telephone wire. If the three selves are working normally and freely together, the low self—at the request of the middle self—can at any time call up the High Self by way of the aka cord and give it a message.[5]

In their healing rituals the kahunas would seek, first, to find *how* we were cut off from High Self. They would start

4. Long, *The Secret Science at Work*, p. 200
5. *Ibid.*, p. 84

by looking for guilt; they would follow by exploring beliefs. Guilt would have come from some belief which middle self was holding, or from some awareness that the "self" was responsible for having hurt someone, self, or other.

If the guilt came from hurting someone it would be necessary to deal with this, in whatever way would make us feel clear; perhaps just going to that person and saying, "I regret—;" and if they could not now be contacted, of using something like Fritz Perls' empty-chair method, as described in the exercises for chapter 2. But often this is complicated because our hurting someone is a retaliation for a hurt. Our feeling of resentment may be "loaded." We may not even be aware for whom it is intended. We are doing it to get even; we want to hurt someone. We may even be turning it in on self.

I believe Jesus' "turn the other cheek" means we only hurt ourselves by hurting another. If an angry "I want to hurt you" feeling cuts us off from our higher living potential then it needs to be cleared by going back to the original I-hate-what-happened feeling, using a nonhurting "I hate—" which expresses itself for what it is, simply a getting it out of *us, not* putting it on another. That is the secret of clearing. Try it. Learn when you are doing that, as opposed to hurting with it. More hurting is only the basis for more guilt.

I believe every guilt has anger behind it, somewhere, not necessarily towards the person we have hurt. That is why I try "I regret—," first, and then explore for hidden anger behind the action which I regret.

Our guilt may come from a belief we have accepted. "It is wrong to—."

> *"If the low self is convinced that the man has been guilty of a wrong act, it feels shame and refuses to contact the High Self in the regular telepathic way across the connecting cord."*[6]

6. *Ibid.*, p. 306

Something feels out of whack. We are not whole. If low self is feeling shame, it may be because low self has accepted a judgment of guilt from middle self. It is middle self who initiated the shame feeling:

> *"Only middle self can sin. The animals in the jungle eat each other without sinning. The low self is an animal even if associated with a middle self, and it is also incapable of sinning."*[7]

Therefore incapable, on its own, of shame.

According to Max Freedom Long's conception of Huna, only what cuts us off from High Self is sin.

Since "only middle self can sin" it appears that the middle self is responsible for the cut-offness. Rather than "low self feeling shame" as Max Freedom Long surmised, I believe it is simply a matter of beliefs, and signals a need for repentance or of examining where we got our beliefs.

But there is another facet to this:

> *The person who feels justified hurting will not be cut off from the High Self.*

Hitler believed himself justified. Was that the source of his tremendous personal power, a power strong enough to convince myriads of his countrymen and women to accept and act on his destructive beliefs about the Jewish race? In the end the power of those with contrary beliefs prevailed, but at what a cost! The Crusaders had tremendous energy for destroying those who did not believe as they did. Seth, in *The Nature of Personal Reality* places strong emphasis on exploring beliefs.

The kahuna knows that the High Self never robs the free will of the other two selves. It seems that middle self is al-

7. *Ibid.*, p. 306

lowed to learn by exerience what damage may be caused by beliefs. Certainly it appears that a lack of guilt is what allows a dictator to contact his power source. Conversely, guilt can be imposed on us by a martyr to exploit or manipulate us. Neither Hitler's lack of guilt nor the imposed guilt of a martyr are very self-actualizing. What is evident from Max Freedom Long's work is that guilt means lack of power and lack of guilt allows a power connection. And that guilt comes from beliefs.

So, as Seth advises, explore your beliefs. They are personal to you and they affect your power connection . . . the power to heal, or the power to destroy. It is not our righteousness in the eyes of others which gives us power, as much as it is our belief in what we are doing. And perhaps the strongest thing we can do, when a Hitler tries to connect us to his beliefs, is to say, "I don't believe you." As so many draft-dodgers did about the war in Viet Nam.

Closely related to this are the feelings: "My heart's into it" or "My heart's not into it." If we are doing something and our heart's not into it we are disconnected from our power source. Our "should-er" is running us, and is doing it through guilt. Where there is guilt there is no power.

Referring back to the Huna teachings of Max Freedom Long and the idea of "the low self being convinced that the man has been guilty" this may refer to a guilt not connected to middle self or to middle self's beliefs, but, through the link to High Self, to a deep awareness of our universal oneness, and to those hurts which result from a negation of that.

Perhaps the more we discover our oneness, as is done at Findhorn, the more guilt we will clear and the less this existential (low self) guilt will exist. Then we will discover power we have not dreamed of, a power that will not be overwhelmed by the power of a Hitler, who gets his from feeling justified in annihilating part of humanity.

I believe there is a relation between power and guilt, and

that it works in all levels of our being, and that, even if only middle self can sin, low self can still be aware of sin which middle self is not yet cognizant of. We may be free to work only with middle self guilt, and perhaps in doing that, we will do enough—for our low self does not sin.

Exercises

1. Using two chairs to make sure of separation of the parts, have middle self (reason) tell low self (feeling) something the self should be doing but isn't:

   (a) Have low self try both: My heart's into it.
   My heart's not into it.

   (b) Feel the weight of each. Is there a strong weight for "My heart's not into it?" Become aware of how strong.

   (c) If middle self still wants to argue against low self's heart, discover if there is a compromise middle self might offer, or a good argument for middle self's case.

   (d) Low self must now either come out with a clear "buzz off" or a clear offer to go along with middle self's wish. Which is it? Trying to go two roads at once only makes us split.

   (e) Try it on and see how the choice feels.

2. *Guilt*

Use the two-chair method. Think of something you feel guilty about.

(a) Think of someone who might have a similar guilt to yours.

(b) Imagine them on the other chair and be their advisor. First have them tell you about the situation with which they feel guilt, while you listen and give advice. Keep going till you come to what feels good to both of you.

(c) Now put yourself on the other chair and give yourself the same advice that you gave your fantasy friend.

3. *Choice*

Think of something you feel you *have to* do. Say "I have to—." Now switch and say "I choose to" for the same thing. Feel the difference.

4. *Forgiveness*

To err is human. To forgive is divine. Find out if you could forgive someone for doing something you would not condone. Explore when and how it would be possible at the same time to hate what someone did and to forgive them for doing it. Under what circumstances could you do that?

The Truth is in the present, and mind is always in the future or the past. So there is no meeting between mind and truth.

—Rajneesh
The Book of Secrets, p. 53

8

FUTURE IS NOT NOW PROMISES

"Tying down our future," I call it.

In the sermon on the mount Jesus is quoted as saying:

"Swear not (an oath) at all; . . . But let your communication be Yea, yea;
Nay, nay; for whatsoever is more than these cometh of evil." (Matt. 5:33-37)

My heart's into it or my heart is not into it. NOW.

Our young people, subconsciously becoming aware of the tying down of the future implied in wedding ceremonies have set up their own rituals. Early in my days as a gestaltist I was asked to the formal wedding of two young friends who had been living together for a year or so. Now they understood better the implications of fidelity than they had when they first met. And they discussed with their Anglican priest what they wanted from the ceremony. The message to the guests was, for me, very meaningful. The priest said that "I will" could not be future. We do not know the future. And that over the years, out of mistrust, we had changed the meaning of the wedding ceremony into a binding of our future, rather than a statement of our now. That all we can say is, "It is my will now."

"It is my will now" is all I can ever truly say. Do not take anyone's promise as more than that. Do not say more than "It is my will now." But feel deeply you mean it. That is what matters. How much is your heart into it? And when someone says to you, "I will" be aware of how much you trust, NOW, what they are saying.

Promises are cheap. They can be used to manipulate: "I promise you something so you will act to me as if I had already given it to you. That makes me more worthwhile." In reality I am trying to tie you to me. Worse still, I am binding my own future also. For all those promises I make, unfilled, are there in my subconscious, weighing on me, unless I deliberately promise with no intention of filling them!

Getting hooked into the expectation that someone will change is related to this. That, also is a tying down of your future. Deal with your discomforts now. Only the change that happens now has meaning.

How often do you hang on, waiting for change that never comes?

I have noticed alcoholics, particularly, making a lot of promises about what they will do. It is my fantasy they have built huge mountains of guilt about the ones they have not kept. Perhaps they could start by looking carefully at each promise they make, in order to:

1. *Discover their motive. What they expect to get out of it.*
2. *Discover how much they believe they are into carrying it out.*
3. *Become more free by making fewer promises.*

There is no exercise to this section except to notice what happens with your promises—yours and your friends'.

It is indeed one of the controversial glories of gestalt that it has, against the entire psychiatric tradition since Freud, with its grim demand for conformity to a joyless conception of adulthood, asserted the nobility and healthiness of the child and the artist.

—Roszak
The Making of a Counter Culture, p. 197

9

CHILDREN

The natural language of children is (low self) ''now'' language, which we, as adults are trying to recover. Adults use middle self language; they tend to rationalize and explain to children. Not that middle self language is not important; it sets us apart from animals.

But we need to be aware that middle self language is not yet children's language; their language is ''feeling:'' love, hate, attraction, repulsion, sadness, joy, etc. So we are not interacting with them when we use middle self language, nor are we likely to be hearing theirs. This makes them feel helpless, frustrated. The farther we get from hearing their needs, the farther they get from hearing their own. Then helplessness becomes a set, a pattern which becomes, I believe, the ''bottomless well'' I spoke of earlier.

Many of us, as adults, are so out of touch with our low selves, our emotional center, that practically all our communication is aboutism. Around us children are starved for contact. We care for them, how healthy they are, what opportunities for growth they have, how adequate their food, and yet we starve them for true contact, which begins with the feeling self.

Most of my work is with people in their twenties or thirties. One of my main delights, and perhaps my greatest, is to see how healthy the effect is on their children, of these adults learning to contact their feeling, and to come from center. Roszak's statement, "the truth is as much a matter of what I am, as of what I know. So I will show you what I am" is particularly applicable in our interaction with children.

Jesus' "Unless you become as little children, you shall in no wise enter the kingdom of heaven," I believe refers to the awareness that the Hunas had, that High Self is reached only through low self; the metaphor "as little children" designating this need, discovered in Huna and in gestalt, to start with low self.

So we do more harm than we know when we destroy this natural bridge to High Self through our over-emphasis on middle self's rationalizing communication.

What, then, are we to do? Ignore middle self? No! Our work as parents is to introduce middle self in such a way that low self feelings are never tramped on, or negated; in this way the two "selves" become integrated. We need to begin by hearing feelings, and by giving a feeling response, adequately and honestly.

When a child wants to stay up in the evening (hates going to bed) we need to hear that first.

"I hate going to bed, now." Let the child know you heard that, so they won't go on and on, trying to get through. I believe real contact requires a sensory contact. Does your voice let the child know? Or your eyes? Or your touch? Whatever your way of making contact, learn when and how your child feels heard by you.

Then the child will be more able to hear you, and what you have to give: "I believe you need to go to sleep now, to have enough for morning." Or maybe that is not your truth; maybe your truth is: "I need quiet now and I want you out of the way. So I am sending you to bed."

In that case let the child know your truth, "I need quiet now," then work this need out in conjunction with the child's needs.

It is important to be firm about your own needs, as well as listening to the child's. The interaction, the hearing of needs on both sides is a growth process for both of you.

Trust in communication depends as much on how you come from center, now, as on how consistently you have come from center in the past. If a parent says "I believe you need to go to sleep now," when they really mean "I can't stand it any longer. I need quiet now" the child gets mixed messages: "parent's concern for me," "parent's not wanting me." And the one they will feel most is parent's not wanting me, the unspoken one. But they are expected to respond to the verbal one. Confusion! Hyperactivity oten results from trying to find a way out of this confusion, a way that can be trusted.

Especially with communicating with children, be wary of you-initiated sentences: "You're too noisy." Judgments can be devastating to a child. It is much "clearer" to give them "I" sentences: "I hate that much noise" or "I can't stand that much noise." Don't push the child with a demand "stop" unless you have first made a contact with the child which will allow the child to trust how you express your needs, as well as how you hear theirs.

If a child is subjected to an overload of you-initiated sentences, or to judgments, they tend to feel like an object, to lose their center as a being; through invalidation of their emotions (you shouldn't feel like that). They tend to feel annihilated. They will signal this annihilation by complaint, stubborn silence or lifeless acquiescence. They may even become "very good" little "objects."

I had a friend whose children were complaining a lot. When she started appreciating that she, herself could say, "I hate—," instead of complaining, she taught this to her children. Now they hear each other. She is very careful to have them understand that it is not them she hates, but something they have done.

She hears, first, that they hate going to bed, and then she

explores her own motives and feelings and plays these back, honestly. They trust her responses. When they whine or complain, she says, "I hear whining. I don't answer to that." Her children have been taught to switch, at that signal, to saying, "I hate—" or "I need—" or whatever their truth, strongly, knowing she *will* listen to that, and will give them hers. An interaction they both trust takes place.

Children come from center, naturally, as animals do. It is our unreal adult patterns that contaminate this flow. Whenever we start communicating to them with rationalizations, not feelings, we need to be aware of what is happening. When we lose touch with the self-regulation of spontaneous adjustment we tend to, as Roszak says, move into a compulsive need to manipulate or control.

Sometimes with children we can get loaded with accumulations of resentments. Then we could say to them: "I'm feeling loaded. I have some clearing to do. I'm going to pretend you're on that chair and I'm going to unload some of these feelings I have been gathering." Even in that kind of unloading be very sure you let the children know you are not hating them, only some of the things they have done. Using an empty chair to represent the child and talking to the "imaginary" child on the empty chair is one way of letting the child be in the process, safely. They understand about pretending someone is there.

I have had playback from parents that this has been very effective for them and for the children. The children have understood what was happening, and have appreciated it. They sense the clearing.

If we are loaded it will be expressed anyway, covertly, in our tightness, in our actions which will appear impatient and unloving, in our voices which will sound harsh or blaming. Children know. These voices make them feel unloved. But if we take time to clear our hating, *cleanly* giving it to them, then they can feel loved. They know when we are clear. They *know* where we are coming from, loaded or loving. What is hard for them to distinguish is the difference between hate and blame. Loaded communication generates blame. Which makes them feel worthless. They can understand we hate some of the things they do; they hate some of the things we do. It is not the hate but the blame which makes them feel worthless.

Also encourage children to put *you* on the empty chair and give you *their* hates. Teach them to be specific, to say just what it is you are doing that they resent. Teach them it is not the person but what the person is doing that they hate. That is important.

I notice that it is easier for us to say, to children, "I am angry" than it is for us to say, "I hate (something they did)." What I hear us doing this way is dodging our "now." In this way we load our children with aboutism but we don't clear. Consciously or unconsciously we want the children to feel guilty or blamed so they will change.

Rather than trusting to just expressing our feelings, and then let go, we want to keep control.

When I give people a sentence that switches from aboutism to now language they usually resist, not wanting to take the risk of letting go of their manipulative controls, of trusting the feasibility of just coming from center with their feelings. I believe that this is because the thing they are most afraid of is trusting their ability to come from center. And rightly so. If we try that and it fails we are faced with our nothingness, our lack of contact with center. When we judge, or blame, or complain, or rationalize, or use put-downs or manipulative "why's" we don't have to risk that; we can stay on top of things. However, then we live in a destructive pattern, creating more destructive patterns for our children. Only when we risk facing our nothingness will we find our center. And begin a generation of real children, who also know their center.

Exercise

As suggested above, use the two-chair method of clearing, and let your child in on the clearing process.

But don't explain. Stay with clear "I hate it when you," "I love when you," "I need—" sentences. *Not* "I need you to—;" *not* "I hate you." Don't try trips on the child, even on the chair.

Through practicing with an empty chair you will learn to communicate more clearly, more directly. And your child will learn to trust you more.

The physicist seeks to understand reality, while the mystic is trained to experience it directly.

—Matthiessen
The Snow Leopard, p. 65

10

DREAMS AND OTHER ROADS

Freud called dreams the royal road to the subconscious. I believe that dreams, the language of low self, are a gateway to the infinite mind and will become increasingly important as the century moves along.

If, as the shamans are aware, low self is our personal power station as well as our link to even higher self, then every link to low self is important to us, and dreams are one of those links.

What we need to learn is how to switch into the language of low self in order that 2-way communication may take place. If we analyze our dreams, or think about them, or interpret them, those ways are not in the language of low self. They belong to middle-self-country. We need to move into the experiential NOW. Both selves understand that language, and miracles of communication can take place.

How do we do this? The following is the way that Fritz Perls taught us. I find Senoi dreamwork using the same principles.

In gestalt dreamwork each part of our dreams is a reflection of ourselves, a part of us interacting with other parts of us. In gestalt dreamwork the medium is the message; the secret is to *become* each part.

Take a scene from the dream. The emotional interaction

of the parts is more important than the story of the dream, so take this scene and become the setting and all its parts, interacting. Each person, each part represents an aspect of you, and your subconscious is choosing these parts and persons to acquaint you with these aspects. As you come to each part, before interacting *become* that part: I am. I am a house. I am old. I remind me of the house I lived in when I was fourteen, etc. Even the house will be expressing some quality of you, perhaps that the feeling of the dream is strongly tied to that time and that place, telling you the roots of the feeling may be found there or at that age.

Take a specific scene from the dream and act out that scene, not sitting passively, talking-about, thinking-about, but letting your whole body express the part, making a dance of it. You can even express a dead person in your dream, by lying still and getting into the feeling of deadness, to discover what that aspect of you means to you. The other parts can express what the deadness means to them. Become your murderers, or monsters or bank robbers with zest. The insights, the releases of buried emotion happen automatically, through being the parts. You may not notice it, your friends are more likely to, that your voice and your body expression will automatically change as you truly get into a part. If this is so a suppressed part of you may be surfacing in order that you may become clearer, more integrated.

Perhaps one part comes up with a powerful expression you would like to use yourself, but do not feel free to do so. Try it on. Take the expression. Play with it. Repeat it. Exaggerate it, until it becomes part of your choices. Then discover if you could validly say that to someone you know, outside the dream.

Perhaps you woke at a scary part. Go back into the dream and see what you could do to go through with it. Continue a fall? Do so. Was there a monster in your dream? Become the monster and do the scaring. Try your monster on some of your friends in the group. The truer you are to a part the more you become integrated. The more release you feel.

By changing the expression of a part while working *in* the experience of the dream, you may give yourself new and valuable response choices in your life and your dreams will know where you need these. Trust them to take you there.

Above all, do not tell the story of your dream. Act it out. *Be* it. Do not describe the parts. *Be* them. After you have acted out key scenes, and have established your parts so you know them better, then you might tell the story of the dream. It may take on newer and fuller meaning. Enjoy your dreams, but don't take them lightly: they may be extremely important. They are low self trying to get through to you.

Exercises

1. Practice working your dreams with the help of a friend or friends who can mirror but not interpret nor lay their own trips on your dream: *They need to be eyes,* seeing movements you might miss, which could be repeated or exaggerated to allow you to get their meaning. Your friends communicate "I see—" (i.e., your hand clenching) and that is all. They can suggest that you exaggerate the action. They do not say: "You are clenching your hand." What is clenching to them may not be clenching to you. Your mirrors simply reflect: *I* see—.

They need to be ears, telling you what they hear in your voice, complaint, judgment, martyr, rebellion, anger, sadness, whatever. They can suggest exaggeration. They do *not* say, "You are being a martyr," they simply say, "I hear—."

They can pick up a key sentence and ask you to repeat it. They can ask who else you would like to say that to, or they could ask you to repeat it to various members of the group.

Above all your friends need to be sensitive, giving only one person's playback on a particular segment of work. Don't get "too many forks in one pickle" as someone so aptly put it in one of my groups.

2. Try to get hold of Stan Fox's Aquarian film, *Madeleine's Dream*, and view it with your friends. You will see Fritz Perls working with a dream. I'm sure the picture will be worth a thousand words.

3. Read the dreamwork sections in *Gestalt Therapy Verbatim* by Fritz Perls.

4. Other roads to the subconscious may be explored through the use of exercises from the following books:

   The Secret Science at Work (see index on uses of the pendulum) by Max Freedom Long

   Dowsing, Techniques and Applications, by Tom Graves

   Your Body Doesn't Lie by John Diamond, M.D.

. . . the so-called "cultured" are always doing that (suppressing hate). But then they become numb, dead.

—Rajneesh
The Book of Secrets, p. 299

11

BREATHING AND VOICE

As dreams are an important link to our subconscious, so also is breathing. If you were to pace (imitate) someone's breathing you could probably identify the emotion they are experiencing. And since breathing is affected by emotion and emotion affects the quality of the voice, the voice reflects the emotional state.

Through breathing, as through dreams, we can move from the subconscious to the conscious. We can breathe, and almost always do, unconsciously; or we can consciously change our breathing patterns. Just as we can benefit by becoming aware of our dream patterns and changing them, so also can we benefit from changing our breathing patterns. Changing our breathing patterns changes our voice.

Fritz Perls told us: "Don't listen to the words, listen to the voice." The words can lie; the voice doesn't. It is easy to get caught up in the words and forget to listen to the voice. The voice will tell you when someone is in their head, cut off from feelings. Then it will be a talking-about voice. A feeling voice will communicate the emotion. Listen to the voice. It will let you know.

Is the voice small and timid? The words may be sounding unafraid but if the voice sounds timid, don't believe the words, believe the voice.

Is the voice dead? That person will probably be looking for some situation or some person from which to suck energy.

Is the voice a lullaby? It may be trying to hypnotize you.

Is the voice booming? or critical? or put-down? Don't expect to be given much room. You may be listening to a self-righteous rebel.

Is the voice going on and on and on? Wanting attention but not risking the expression of its own emotion? You could get swamped in aboutism. Or sucked into supplying energy for that person.

Does the voice complain? It will have a yang-yang sound, whining. It will try to make you responsible for making its world right. And it will resist strongly finding out what it can do for itself. Its theme song is: The World's not Right. Don't get sucked into its problems. They could be endless.

It may be a martyr's voice: "I have done so much for you (or others)." You don't owe a martyr anything. You can give to them. You do not owe. They are trying to buy you. Beware.

Is the voice syrupy? Don't trust it.

Is the voice accusing? This one is also avoiding its emotions. It will be good at getting your defense up; then it will build its case. Don't defend, nor join sides with it.

Is the voice self-righteous, judgmental? It is also avoiding emotions. Notice it starts its sentences with You, They, It is, etc. Challenge it to make "I am" statements.

Does the voice question a lot? It may be trying to control, to manipulate, to pin you down, making you come to it and at the same time writing the rules of how you do it. Ask it to make statements out of its questions, i.e., "Are you coming now?" into "I'm impatient to get going."

Does it cry in order to get sympathy? Or are the tears a genuine expression of pain or grief? Listen.

Sometimes just working with either voice or breath or both will release stuck emotions. Then the voice will change. After a gestalt workout when a connection has been made, the voice will sound richer, stronger, more resonant. Alive. Listen for this. Incidentally, after a workout which connects and finishes with a feeling, colors also will be brighter. When the voice is dead the colors are dull.

Exercises

1. Whenever you recognize, in yourself, the voices listed above try coming from center with clear feeling statements: I hate—, I love—, I believe—, etc.; let yourself connect to the feeling and express it, fully.

2. To work with breathing exercises, use any of the exercises from the following books:

   Awareness Through Movement, Feldenkrais

   Toning, Laurel Keyes

   Science of Breath, Ramacharaka

   Breathing, the ABC's, Carol H. Speads

   Yoga, Twenty-eight Day Exercise Plan, Richard Rittleman

The Way to Vibrant Health, Alexander Lowen and Leslie Lowen

3. Repeat exercise 4 from exercises for *The Hole or Bottomless Well* chapter (page 51).

4. Move about, repeating the sounds "Ha, Ho" with your whole body taking part. Make a dance of it.

BIBLIOGRAPHY AND SUGGESTED READING

Bandler, Richard, and John Grinder, *frogs into princes*, Real People Press, 1979.

David, William, *The Harmonics of Sound, Color & Vibration*, DeVorss & Co., 1980.

Delaney, Gayle, *Living Your Dreams*, Harper & Row, 1979.

Diamond, John, M.D., *Your Body Doesn't Lie*, Warner Books, 1979.

Feldenkrais, Moshe, *Awareness Through Movement*, Harper & Row, 1972.

Graves, Tom, *Dowsing Techniques and Applications*, 1976.

Hittleman, Richard, *Yoga, Twenty-eight-day Exercise Plan*, Bantam Books, 1978.

Keyes, Laurel E., *Toning, the Creative Power of the Voice*, DeVorss & Co., 1974.

Levine, Sylvia and Joseph Kenig (Ed.), *Why Men Rape, Interviews with Convicted Rapists*, MacMillan of Canada, 1980.

Long, Max Freedom, *The Secret Science at Work* (1953) and *The Secret Science Behind Miracles* (1948), DeVorss & Company.

Lowen, Alexander and Leslie, *The Way to Vibrant Health*, Harper & Row, 1977.

Maslow, Abraham, *Towards a Psychology of Being*, Van Nostrand Reinhold, 1968.

Matthiessen, Peter, *The Snow Leopard*, Bantam Books, 1978.

Perls, Fritz, M.D., *Gestalt Therapy Verbatim*, Real People Press, 1959; Bantam Books, 1971.

Rajneesh, Bhagwan Shree, *The Book of Secrets*, Harper & Row, 1977. *Only One Sky*, E. P. Dutton, 1976.

Ramacharaka, Yogi, *The Science of Breath*, Yoga Publication Society, 1904.

Roberts, Jane, *The Nature of Personal Reality: A Seth Book,* Prentice-Hall, 1974.

Roszak, Theodore, *The Making of a Counter Culture*, Doubleday, 1969.

Speads, Carola H., *Breathing, the ABC's*, Harper & Row, 1978.

Magazine Articles:
"An Interview with the Simonton's," *New Age Magazine*.

"The Joy (Grief, Love, Hate, Anger, Sex, Reverence) of Music," *Human Behavior,* Vol. 6, No. 4, April 1977.